What Is for DINNER?

by Donna Foley

PEARSON

Scott Foresman

Editorial Offices: Glenview, Illinois • Parsippany, New Jersey • New York, New York
Sales Offices: Needham, Massachusetts • Duluth, Georgia • Glenview, Illinois
Coppell, Texas • Ontario, California • Mesa, Arizona

What **crops** grow near where you live? In the summer many fresh fruits and vegetables might grow in your area. Some of these foods are sold at a farmer's market.

At the farmer's market you can buy food that is grown by local farmers. You might buy tomatoes, peppers, apples, and onions in the summer. In the winter it is too cold for some crops to grow in some places. There may not be a farmer's market.

In the winter you might buy your food at the grocery store because the farmer's market may be closed. The grocery store sells food from all over the country. Farmers, or **producers**, from warmer places ship their foods to grocery stores in colder places.

4

Some foods may not be grown near you. They grow only in warmer places. These foods are shipped to your grocery store. **Consumers** can find most foods at the grocery store all year long.

Even if a food does not grow where you live, you might receive it as a gift. Pecans and peaches grow in South Carolina, and oranges and grapefruits come from Florida. What a fun way to enjoy treats from faraway places!

You and your family can eat food that comes from near and far. Food that is grown all over the world can arrive in your kitchen for you to enjoy.

Glossary

consumer someone who buys and uses
goods

crop a kind of plant that people grow and use

producer someone who makes or grows
something